SBL
ASk

Uncut
Confetti

JOHN HEGLEY

with drawings by the author

Methuen

First published by Methuen 2006

10 9 8 7 6 5 4 3 2

Copyright © John Hegley

Methuen Publishing
8 Artillery Row
London SWIP 1RZ

www.methuen.co.uk

ISBN 10: 0-413-77570-4

ISBN 13: 978-0-413-77570-2

A CIP catalogue record for this book
is available from the British Library

Designed by Bryony Newhouse

Printed and bound in Great Britain by
St Edmundsbury Press Ltd, Bury St Edmunds, Suffolk

First edition

CONTENTS

A MAKE-OVER MISTAKE   1

BABY AT WORK   2

BANNED   3

BEACH   4

BELIEFS AND PROMISES   6

CARDBOARD COMFORT   8

DOMINOES   9

EXTREEMIST   10

FOOTSTEP   11

FOR ANNE   12

FOR THERAPEUTIC PURPOSES   14

GETTING IN A LAVA   15

GLASGOW WINDOW   17

GOOD LOOKING   18

GRANDDAD'S GLASSES   20

GREATEST ITS   22

HIS LITTLE BIT ON THE SIDE   23

ILKLEY TO CARLISLE, IN STAGES   24

LONDON TO MANCHESTER   25

LONG LOST   27

MESSIAH   28

MINOTAUR   30

MONKEY BUSINESS   31

MORNING SICK   33

MORNINGSIDE AND BEYOND   34

MR COOPER CONTINUED   37

MUNCH   47

NINE MEN   49

ON PAPER   51

ORPHEUS AND THE ANIMALS   52

QUESTIONS   53

REVISITING HOME   55

SHIFTING IT   57

SMALL SISTER   59

STICK MAN   60

THAILAND 2001   62

THE CLIMB   63

TONY AND THE FISH   65

TRAMPING   66

23.1.00: 11.40 A.M.   68

2B 2½   69

WAY OUT   71

WILD BUNCH   74

ZANZIBAR   75

ZEN DAD   84

For those who were concerned, watchful and generous during a time of wrong-headedness, thank you.

UNCUT CONFETTI

A MAKE-OVER MISTAKE

There's a photo of my father, I think it's Monte Carlo, I'd say the 1930s. A young man fired up and dashing, in spatted shoes and cravat. In the Seventies and *his* sixties, when he was retired, I thought it would be a good idea if he could be a little more trendy. Just because he was getting old, didn't mean he had to look like he'd lost it. So, he and I went to Bristol City centre and bought tank tops, and purple flared trousers. Also, at my behest, he grew his sideburns. When the changes were complete, I didn't say anything because I didn't want to offend him, but I thought we had made an error. And perhaps because he didn't want to offend me either, only very gradually did he ease back into the man he had once been.

BABY AT WORK

She is one.
She is having fun.
Everything's a skittle
or in the wrong place.
Surfaces are to be cleared.
Milk is to be spilt
not cried about.
Crying is for getting stuff:
attention, biscuits, the pencil full of poem.
The soil in the houseplants
is there to be spread
around the carpet.
Glasses don't belong on tables, or the face,
and parents do not belong in the bed.

BANNED

The wedding of Simon and Janet had to be postponed at the last minute, on account of a technicality.

Simon and Janet were going to get married
but they never got married instead.
They still went down to the Rose and Crown
which they'd chosen for the spread.
It took a while to plan it
and Simon and Janet still went ahead
with the sandwiches and vol-au-vents,
with the beer and the bits of bread.
The nuptials were put on hold
but the victuals were fed.
To this Aussie and Pomme,
to this femme and this homme,
here's to the newly unwed.

BEACH

On the beach,
with my baby,
on the beach.
My baby's in the buggy
on the beach.
I'm pushing my baby
in the buggy,
pushing my baby
down to reach
a deckchair that I like the look of
which is flapping out all stripy, nicely,
nicely, on the beach.

Making sure my baby's sorted,
sunscreen, sun hat
and that.
Got to get that brolly re-positioned.
Got to keep that UV thwarted.
We're past the time when we have got to keep
our baby's head supported,
but we're not yet at the flowering of speech.
I'm docking with my deckchair.
My baby's got a pushchair.
We've got the one chair each.

I push and pull my deck chair,
as I feel the need to lay me back as far as I can reach.
What the heck, yeah?
The payment gets no higher
with the lower that you reach:
I want my deckchair on those last two notches
… my baby's gone to sleep.
Buenos noches.

BELIEFS AND PROMISES

I believe in dog, the rather all bitey.
I believe that saying I will do something
makes me less likely to do it.
I believe that a bus is less well served by a single operator
    than if you crew it
but I still believe in thanking the driver when I get off,
although if the exit is through a middle door
you can't make eye contact with your thanks
unless you go down to the cabin before leaving
which all seems a bit much for this small courtesy.
I believe that Jesus would have been a smoker.
I believe that Buddha would have been a good goalie.
I believe there is a greater whole which I am part of.
I believe in not ending sentences with prepositions.
I believe that rules are there to suggest the possibility of
    breaking them,
but I don't believe that rules are made to be broken
because that's just another rule.

I promise to remember that you are beautiful.
I promise to remember that I too am beautiful.
I promise to be less negative and paranoid,
who are you looking at?
I promise to sing.

I promise to dance.
I promise to love.
I promise to kiss.
I promise to think before I speak.
I promise to speak before I think.
I promise to spink before I theak.
I promise to know when to stop.

CARDBOARD COMFORT

My baby's full of baby,
she's going to be a mum.
I watch her tummy undulate,
and feel for our new chum.
I've made a tummy-megaphone
down which I like to sing,
but whether or not the noise is welcome
that's another thing.

DOMINOES

I like a game of dominoes,
wood on wood,
wholesome and good.
I like the black clacking
heralding a game's beginning.
I like to lay them
end to end.
I like to play them
with my friend.
And I like winning.

EXTREEMIST

When he mentioned that he helped out with an
    environmental charity,
he was asked which one.
He identified it as one which conserved ancient
    woodland.
When it was suggested that there might be more
    urgent causes,
he asked, 'Like what?'
'Like caring for the needy child,' he was advised.
He indicated that children did not last as long as trees
and nor were they as beautiful.

FOOTSTEP

I first put

my foot

on the stage

in the Luton Central

Library, at the age

of twelve.

The play was

The Merchant of Venice.

I liked the bit

when they looked

in the three boxes

and each one

had a rhyme in it.

But generally

I preferred

Dennis the Menace.

FOR ANNE

You hadn't let me come to you before,
because you hadn't wanted me to see you unwell.
But now, it couldn't be helped.
Because it was now or, maybe, never.
And so, I was invited to your hospital bedside.
Anne, when our friendship began
we suspected
it might span only a short while.
In that meeting
we got to smile,
squeeze palms,
and share the pleasure of my hand-operated dog,
which I'd had since it was a puppet.
I showed you the pink-penned badge
given me by my daughter.
You told me to never take it off,
then whispered me to see your own girl
through, what you bravely referred to as,
this difficult time.
You were from Leeds,
and you looked after people's needs,
no messing.
You showed me the photos of the blessing
which you and your gentle John received on the ward.

The images of you and your close ones
celebrating the occasion with the staff,
who had found the office hole-punch
and poured its contents over you both.
A marvellous, inspired and inspiring piece
        of improvisation.
The deepest, and most humbling, of hospital care.
Anne, I'll remember you, lovely,
with the world's best-ever confetti
in your hair.

FOR THERAPEUTIC PURPOSES

I have not been quite right in the head.
Like a balding tyre, I've been losing my grip.
I have been given various medications
to help me cope:
anti-depressants,
anti-psychotics.
And my brother has given me
a skipping rope.

GETTING IN A LAVA

The Frenchman, Patrice, is preceded
by a reputation for mapping and snapping
    volcanoes.
I am told it is not his work, but his passion.
Getting to meet the man
around a French mealtime table
at the home of his sister, Cecile,
he intimates that canyons
also get him and his camera going.
I indicate the steep sides
which canyons and volcanoes have in common.
His sister indicates a brother always reeling
on the edge of a precipice of some sort.
A man on the edge.

Fruit is offered for dessert.
Patrice proceeds
to pare the apple peel with his pocket knife,
and as he uses it again
to divide the flesh,
it triggers a forgotten flash of my father.
Him sat at our meal-time table with his own
    pen knife,
generously giving me the best slice

from hands cracked to angry canyons
and salved with Vaseline.
Dad, you were sometimes ready to erupt,
but in spite of any scalding spanking which
        you gave me
I was never in any doubt
that you would unquestioningly sacrifice
the rest of your life
to save me.

GLASGOW WINDOW

Awaiting the shuttle bus
from Glasgow Central
to take us
to Queen Street Station,
across the road's divide
a man inside a shop window.
I thought, he must know me,
or why else would he be waving?
Further scrutiny invests the gent's gesture
with other meaning:
he is not waving,
but window cleaning.

GOOD LOOKING

You look good, oh yes, I can tell,
not just what you look like,
how you look as well.
You look good, ok, the way you see,
it's a departure from the common travesty.
You look good, alright, you've got an eye,
you see it plain, your sort's in very short supply.
You can see it in 3D
and you've not even got the glasses,
you look good
and you look good with the narcissistic problem.
You look good, aye aye,
you look good.
Through your peephole
you see people
as you should.
You look good, yeah, yeah,
you look *very* good.
You look at the trees
and these do not obscure the wood.
You look good, mmm
you look good.

You see the Christmas that is in the Christmas pud.
You look good, yeah, yeah,
you look good,
and I'd give you more examples
if I could.

GRANDDAD'S GLASSES

Granddad's going underground tomorrow,
in a mahogany box,
it was his favourite timber.
We've made the requiem arrangements
and we'll even be able to find a home
for granddad's socks and pyjamas,
but when someone passes away
there's always a problem or two:
how we gonna break it to granddad's doggie,
and what we gonna do about granddad's glasses?
What we gonna do about granddad's glasses?
He didn't like to see things wasted.
What we gonna do about granddad's glasses?
He didn't like to see things being thrown away.
Maybe somebody could use the frame
but it's always a shame to break a pair up,
a bus pass you can just tear up,
but you can't just tear up
your granddad's glasses.
At least grandma had the sense to leave him
before he finished breathing,
you need a little joke at times like these
and granddad would have had us all having a
        knees up

but, what we gonna do about granddad's glasses?

They won't be going underground with granddad,
he didn't believe in telly after death.
Opportunity no longer knocks for granddad,
he was running for the bus, when he ran right out
　　　of breath.
And just to add one final twist
a postcard came for him this morning,
they only mis-spelt his name slightly
otherwise they put it so politely,
Dear Sir or Madam your new spectacles are ready
　　　for collection.
What we gonna do about granddad's glasses?
I don't mean the ones he kept his teeth in.
What we gonna do about granddad's glasses?
The ones he won't be going underneath in.
It isn't easy to realise
that granddad's eyes are closed forever.
Now I know what a farce is.
Now I know what a farce is.
What we gonna do without granddad?
What we gonna do without that grand old daddy,
and what we gonna do about granddad's empty glasses?

GREATEST ITS

It's the poems in my pencil.
It's the tango in my heart.
It's the bang which starts the sack-race
when the cactus blows the red balloon apart.
It's the longer standing friendship
which turns latterly to love.
It's the glove-puppet before the hand's inside.
It's the halfpenny that will shortly be acquainted with
    the shove.
It's the strength we don't know we possess
until the pressure is applied.
It's the holding of your hand
that makes me happy in the morning,
on a misty day
and on our way to school.
It's the murmurings of genius
I've seen when you are drawing.
It's the news of your new distance
down the swimming pool on Fridays.
It's your plinking the piano in the home.
It's each time you call me Daddy
even when you're getting mad
because I'm pulling on your tangles
with the comb.

HIS LITTLE BIT ON THE SIDE

Now and then she liked to give
her hubby something funny with his grub.
In his packed lunch
she put a punch line,
chucking him a chuckle
in his lunchtime,
something that would tickle
with the cheese and pickle sandwiches.
From time to time
she packed a punch line,
with an orange
or satsuma from the sun,
in his packed lunch,
a pithy punch line.
Why should Christmas crackers have all the fun?
She wanted to know, she wanted to know
the difference between God and a Potato
… *God may be an all seeing*
infinite, omnipresent being,
but he's not as good as potatoes are
with chives and mayonnaise,
and spuds don't get much of a look in on Songs of Praise.
But they should do.
They ought to.

ILKLEY TO CARLISLE, IN STAGES

I – ILKLEY TO LEEDS

The fare was ninety pence. I gave the conductor a one pound coin and he gave me my change in one and two pence pieces with a certain vindictive pleasure. I am sometimes tempted to say that people who do this can keep their troublesome coins, but I think they'd see this as profit rather than protest.

II – LEEDS TO SKIPTON

I buy my onward ticket with a fifty pound note. The man at the ticket office holds it up to the light, then says, 'I wouldn't know a forgery if I saw one.' I admire his humour and humanity.

III – SKIPTON TO CARLISE

This includes the Settle to Carlisle journey, reputedly the most striking scenic railway route in the country, and the reason for my circuitous journey. Unfortunately the visibility is thirty feet.

LONDON TO MANCHESTER

The man opposite has got his shoes off and his feet on the seat opposite him. Although the socks look quite clean, I keep suspecting there is a warm cheeselike whiff about the compartment. I'm hoping the inspector comes by and has a word. If I ever put my feet on a vacant berth, I always place paper underneath, which has seemed to be an acceptable attention in the eyes of rail staff members.

Perhaps I should report this man to the guard whom I've glimpsed only briefly. Hold on though, we've just come out of Rugby, so I could have travelled all this way without payment, which tends to make me think the guard will be the kind of man not too bothered about minor foot infringements, in which case I won't report old toe-wiggler there, so this time he's fortunate.

Hello, I've just looked up from writing this and he's got his shoes back on. Quite a nice looking pair of brogues actually, very worn, mind. Now I've suddenly smelled alcohol breath, it must be this new bloke sat in front of me, who got on at Rugby. Is the odour bad enough for me to move? I'll definitely go if he's sick. Unless he does it in a sick bag, in which case I might remain here out of respect for his considerate attitude. There's a right stink, though. The trouble is, if you start moving with a biggish piece of luggage when you're miles away from the last station stop, people wonder about you. Where are we now? Was that Stoke or Stafford? Just caught the St… Here comes the guard at last, now where's my ticket?

Here we are.

'Is it best to change at Crewe or Preston, officer?'

'Oh, Crewe'.

He says it very assuringly. *Very* firmly. I think it's quite lucky for Socky that he's put his shoes on, actually.

LONG LOST

My first step
out of the house
 in long trousers.
My first
step with my trousers
touching my shoes.
 My first step in trousers
  over my knees,
   like my dad's.
    Before long, I would miss
     getting these knees dirty,
     and miss the conkers
       in my pocket
     and the marbles.
      At the big boys' school
       my marbles were lost.
        Long trousers,
         long face,
          short change.

MESSIAH

This Messiah walks into a bar
and asks for a drink of tap water.
'Why don't you *buy* a drink for a change,
instead of changing water into one?'
says the barman.
'Buy one? What with?' asks the Messiah.
'How come you never have any money?'
'Because I don't believe in it.'
'What *do* you believe in?'
'I believe in *you*. I *love* you.'
'Don't give me that,
you buy a drink or you get out.'
'Oh, come on, what does a drink of water cost?'
'It costs me labour to pour it.
You take up space to drink it,
then I have to wash the cup up after you.
And what if you break it?
Who pays then?'
'I could mend it.'
'Perform a miracle, you mean?
And have everyone crowding around
      in amazement
and *not buying drinks*? No thanks.
Out.'

MINOTAUR

In the myth,
in the deep-down maze of the cave,
he went to find the Minotaur.
And before he went
he took a reel of twine:
a trick to traipse the return trip
back to the world of sense and sunshine.
It was sound thinking:
be enticed by new chance and challenge,
but keep in touch
with your place of origin.
Don't let your past be lost,
or it'll cost
your future.

MONKEY BUSINESS

When I was a boy
our family went for a day enjoying the seaside.
After the beach, wandering together up a town street
a man with a camera asked me to hold his monkey.
I giggled at the friendly, bony, jerky creature.
As I showed his clambering pet to my sister,
the man took a photo.
He said he would post the developed picture to
  my dad,
who could then return payment if he decided
  to keep it.
My dad was someone who did not care to spend
  where it wasn't needed.
For instance, to save on paying a barber
he always gave us our hair-cuts himself.
So he told the man with the camera
that he had not asked for a photograph of a monkey
and did not intend to pay money
for what he did not want.
The man said he would send the photo anyway,
if my dad wrote down our address.
My dad answered that if the chap wished to do this,
  that was his own business.
Days after the day out had been forgotten

the photo arrived.
I looked at the scene and did not think about the
      funny little monkey,
only about the embarrassing coat which I was wearing.
The coat that did not fit me.
It was the coat I called *the horrible shorty mac.*
The monkey went in a photo album
which I hoped would stay forever shut.
I did not realise, that much worse than my coat
was my haircut.

MORNING SICK

I've felt sickly since this morning.
Might be something I've eaten.
Mid-evening outside the Everyman Theatre,
leaving the taxi,
the driver asks me,
'Who's on tonight?'
Feebly, I say, 'It's me.'
Cheerily he calls, 'Break a leg,
that's what they say, isn't it?'
'Yes, it is,' I reply, still feeble.
'You'll be cool,' he affirms.
All day, I've been feeling more flushed than cool,
flushed at both ends.
But, approaching the Stage Door,
I think that if anywhere can make me feel cool,
you'll,
Liverpool.

MORNINGSIDE AND BEYOND

At a dinner in Lisbon after a performance for the British Council, I am told that there is a Saint Andrew's Day dinner in the city, at which I would be most welcome to make the Toastmaster's speech. I am asked if I have any Scottish connections as backup to such an invitation.

I answer that my father was born in France, to a French mother, so I could invoke the Auld Alliance between the two countries. Less tenuously, perhaps, I am from the same island as the Scots.

On an occasion when I was speaking with an Irish poet, I asked if she had any plans to visit my home city of London. She answered that she didn't 'get over to *the other island* very often'. At a stroke, internal borders dissolved. Manchester was no longer in the north of England. It was nearer the middle of *the island*. A little to the south actually.

I have a suspicion that geology not only has an influence on what is mined in a region, but also what is *mind* – in the sense of having a direct influence on the human personality. As a crystal is suspected to have a physical effect, so, I propose, do chalk and granite. Rock strata rarely obey national boundaries. National fragmentation is a human construction which rarely exists in the landscape: to be English is not to be utterly English. We are all islanders.

Extract from Toastmaster's Address at the St Andrew's Ball – Lisbon, November 2002

Bon noyt, and thank you for honouring me with the opportunity to give this toast to Scotland.

As you've probably guessed, I'm English. I'm also an old pal of things Caledonian: heather, gorse, salt and sauce, mickle, muckle, buckled shoes, the Stone of Scone, *skean dhus*, Pontius Pilate … yes, the infamous Roman hailed from Scotland. His father was an Augustan envoy of peace to the British king Metallanus. Fortingall on the northern tip of Loch Tay was the birthplace of Pontius. Something of which some of you may not be conscious.

Seeking information about Saint Andrew himself, I have discovered that certain of his bones – arm, knee, finger and tooth – were brought to Scottish shores from Constantinople by the monk Regulus, who had a dream, or vision, telling him to bring the Saint's bones to 'the ends of the earth'.

As a tribute to the Auld Alliance, I would now like to juggle with potatoes whilst performing a poem in French …

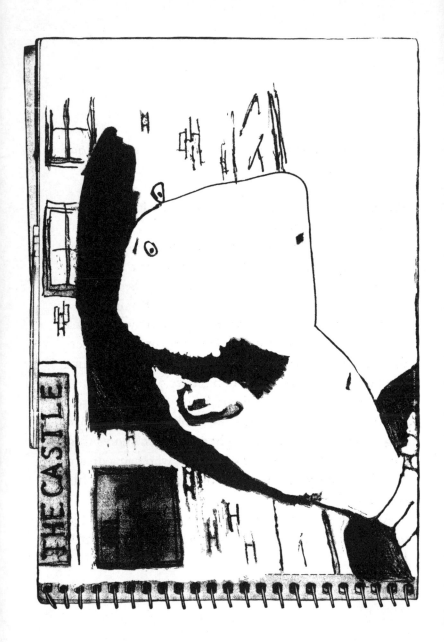

MR COOPER CONTINUED

This piece began as a response to the poem 'Mr Cooper' by Anthony Thwaite. The poem's narrator recounts a visit to a Manchester pub in the 1960s. He finds a jeweller's card left on a shelf above a lavatory urinal. Turning it over, he discovers the words MR COOPER DEAD written in thick pencil. He leaves the pub disconcerted by this stark reminder of mortality.

With a less formal structure, my own piece takes up the voice in the poem, in 1960s' Manchester.

So, he was dead,
the card had said.
Back in the hotel
that calling card
was on my mind, indelibly,
such hard words
for so soft a pencil,
so few words
to cancel
Mr Cooper.
Who was he?
An ardent call within me said:
find out what you can

about the man,
pick up the thread.
And so next day,
washed, brushed and breakfasted,
other work which I had planned would wait,
I'd be a Mr Cooper snooper
of sorts.
So where would my investigating eye first fall?
The jeweller should be worth a call, obviously,
but it's a trait
of mine
to mine
where it's less obvious:
oblivious
to the obvious,
that's me.
Occasionally.

That Manchester morning
the Spring was in the air
and in my step,
the schlep of discovery ahead.
In a public library reading room
I grazed the local press,
unearthing the only Mr Cooper
reported meeting maker
in the region round that time.
A reference volume rendered an address.
I dipped out into the afternoon,
found a bus to Hulme.
Our conductor knew the street

and advised me of a short cut.
I dipped off in the advised direction but
quickly went askew.
I could have bought a map of course,
but more can sometimes happen
with the littler we do.
Although, on this occasion
I just spent a long time wandering aimlessly.

Back on track,
the designated door I knocked,
Mrs Cooper wasn't shocked.

She understood my need to trace him,
felt it must be fate,
asked me in,
his full length photo leant above the grate.
I complimented her former husband's looks,
admired his hat.
'His hats were always top,' she opted.
I wondered what was that
sat at his photoed feet?
Was it a huge potato?
'No, it's a dog,'
our dialogue continued.
'It's out in the kitchen as we speak,
he kept it like a king.'

'A King Edward?' I suggested.
She suggested I curtail potato talk
and take the creature for a walk.

The kitchen door open,
the dog streaked through.
'I can barely bear to look at him,
it brings to mind his master!' she sighed.
'... Would you care to have the dog yourself?
He's got a licence, he's injected
and he's wormed.'
I explained my home was short on space,
'I'll take him for that walk, though,'
I confirmed.

I decided to walk the animal substantially.
An eight or nine hour job, I reckoned:
give Mrs Cooper an obvious break.

As I approached her porch a second time,
a church bell chimed the ten,
I'd had to take the beast
shouldered, for at least the last two hours.
The door opened, the dog barked.
The creature and me
came through to the settee.
'Thanks for doing him,
he likes a nice long one,
but who doesn't,' she observed jokingly.
'I've made you a packed lunch, by the way.'
It seemed late for packed lunching
but any foodstuff was welcome enough,

I'd not touched a crumb since brekky.
A reccy of my parcel
revealed an orange
and some silver foil enclosing no more than a sliver of egg.
Mrs Cooper explained
that it had previously contained bread
and full filling,
but she'd eaten it.
'You've still got the *idea* of a sandwich though,' I was advised,
which I found not depressing,
but thrilling.
I'd been unwilling to address my drawn-ness
to this woman.
But now I'd stop,
for she, too, was top.
She had an expansive point of view
which you could just smell.
She had the stench of anarchist enchantment about her.
Yes, she reeked havoc.

She offered further food,
'Have a fig roll…'
'Lovely, yes, thank you.'
I wasn't mad keen on the fig roll scene
but I didn't want to be rude, and who does?
And why?
'Think of it as your little bit on the side,' she said.
She told me how her husband
had once been a hat-blocker in Stockport.
'…The trade's dying though,' she added,
with evident pain at mortality's mention.

'I'm sorry about your husband, Mrs Cooper.
May I ask you, how did he die?'
She told me that he'd choked on a fig roll.
I told her I was sorry.
She said, 'It wasn't horrible,
he died laughing, you know.'
'… laughing and choking,' I offered,
'… that's right,' she accepted.

I must admit,
my fire was well and warmly lit, by the woman.
But as I tucked into my imaginary sandwiches
I became resistant.
No, no – don't go down that way,
you know where there's a spark
the dark is not far distant,
you know that heaven is twinned with hell.

You know that it can only
go lonely …
'Don't be so stupid,'
reproved the Cupid within,
and I made my move.
'Can I kiss you, Mrs Cooper?'
'Call me Alice,' she answered plainly.
Our swelling kiss completed, she said,
'Don't do that again.'

I had hoped she might have said:
Move up to Manchester,
I've been waiting for you.
Move up to Manchester,
that's what you've got to do.
More love to Manchester,
that's what you've got to bring – your love to Manchester,
make more of Manchester sing.
Move up to Manchester,
come and share my abode.
Move up to Manchester,
up the Liverpool Road.
Move up to Manchester,
come and be where I am,
Move up to Manchester,
or at least to Altrincham.
But she didn't.

'He was so many things to me,' she confided.
'He was the lover of my life,
He was my fresh tomato ketchup,

He was the mustard on my pie,
He was the eye of my potato. Yes, potato,' she smiled.
'He was the life and party of my soul,
He was the sole priest of my amazement,
He was the line of my horizon,
He was my stuff bought from the buffet,
He was my cup of borrowed sugar,
He was my favourite Liquorice Allsort,
He was my grass from Honolulu,
He was my dog dirt of good fortune,
He was my unexpected downpour,
He was the apple of the orders of my doctor.'

I asked her, 'Was he your funny little facecloth?
Was he your corrugated ironing board?'
Mrs Cooper replied
that he was many things,
but not these two.

MUNCH

I want to give you
at least a hundred bouquets.
You're the yeast of my consciousness,
you make my consciousness raise.
We all have our feeble days
and these are mine,
please forgive me
for thinking you're divine.
I'm only human
and I just have to dream,
I'm only a human
you must know what I mean.
Edvard Munch would have liked your face,
I reckon he'd have given you a lot of canvas space.
Edvard Munch. Edvard Munch.

I see you on the boulevard
and in the cafés.
You're never there, of course,
you're somewhere else in the maze.
Edvard Munch would have made you scream,
you are a true bohemian.
And I'm only human,
I have to have a moan,

a lonely human,
please don't leave me alone.
Edvard Munch was a human too,
I reckon he'd have seconded
a big thumbs up to you,
Edvard Munch.

NINE MEN

Today I made a last-minute decision to go and see Luton play QPR who are higher in the league than we. I thought it might be a good one to go to. Arriving at the ground it was sold out. I thought, I'll see if I can find my old school chums Andrew Cornelius and Charlie, who always drink in the same nearby clubhouse before the game. If I can't get in, I can at least say hello and then buy a radio and listen to the match on the local BBC station, which I can't get at home in London. And maybe I'll stand outside the ground for extra atmospherics. So, I go up towards the clubhouse, it's 2.45 and I see the old friends coming down the pavement. For a bit of fun I hide behind a tree trunk and jump out into their path and loudly ask them, 'Do you want some aggro?' Charlie is more surprised than Andrew Cornelius and he says I nearly gave him a heart attack. After a few yards of chat, I tell them that I have no ticket. Fortunately Andrew Cornelius says he just happens to have a spare. Inside the ground some harsh refereeing results in Luton having a man sent off in each half. From the assembled, a song arises: 'Nine men, we've only got nine men'.

QPR – better placed in the league, and now with a bigger team – still fail to gain the advantage. 'Nine men, nine men,' the Luton voices intone and when the stoppage-time board signals four minutes of added-on football, the home fans' instinct is not Oh no, it's four more minutes to stick it out, but Oh yes! Four more minutes to see the splendid triumph of the few. And from the crowd once more, a reiterating of the strange elation, 'Nine men, nine men'. Then the whistle. A journey's end. A pilgrimage completed. No goals, but deepest joy. On the wooden steps down from the main stand, I renew my footballing faith to the sympathetic ears of Andrew Cornelius: football is that which is greater than us, but that which we are part of. The Town crowd can be tough, but on this occasion disgust and disgruntlement are transformed into a celebration of exceptional adversity overcome. The miracle of the sorely depleted, the sure in sight when all at sea. The wonder of the underdog, the down but not yet done for. The Nine Men. Amen.

ON PAPER

She's sat with me here at the table
she isn't yet able to speak,
she's throttling into her bottle
she's only a month and a week.
I mixed her milk yesterday evening
to make up her milk from the breast,
it's twenty past three in the morning,
she's wearing her sleep-suit and vest.
I'm writing this poem one handed
the other is feeding the muse,
she's just had a wee bit of winding
and over my poem she spews.

ORPHEUS AND
THE ANIMALS

I was slack,
I looked back.
Now, I've nothing to took forward to.

Now, you creatures
are my teachers.
You give me a lesson in how
to live all my life in the now.

Mind you,
when I feel like a bit of a chat,
you're useless.

QUESTIONS

Is poetry dying?
Poetry is death-defying. Wide awake and pleased as punch, take the biscuit out to lunch, it's all around. We can't just dump it. We're poetry bound. Like it or lump it.

What's the difference between poetry and performance poetry?
One's more for sitting on the page, one's more for someone to stand on a stage with. There's poetry that requires reading, there's poems that demand more of a din. I've got a poem which needs the paper it's written on to be folded into an aeroplane and I've got others which need throwing in the bin.

Why do you write so much about dogs?
When I was about three, I kept a grey stuffed toy dog with shiny beady eyes. I called him Pet. He was one of three animals in the little animal club I used to cuddle at night. The other two were a lamb and a pony, but they had no names, except lamb and pony.

Do you have an obsession with potatoes?
When I was about three, I also kept a pet potato but the others wouldn't let him join the animal club.

What is your favourite saying or proverb?
Love your enemies.

What is your favourite chat-up line?
You must be an enemy, because I love you.

If you could change one thing about yourself, what would it be?
My deeply treacherous nature.

What annoys you most about drivers?
Their cars.

How does it feel being a poet?
Like a pet with a collar.

Poet, with literature

REVISITING HOME

I spent the age of seven or eight
to almost seventeen
in a bungalow in Luton
which my mum kept very clean.
Monday was a washing day
and Tuesday was as well,
and Wednesday was, and Friday,
it was sometimes hard to tell the days apart,
it was sometimes hard to tell each other
what was in your heart.

I spent the swinging sixties
a-swinging to and fro
on a swing in the back garden
of the Luton bungalow.
Beside my father's rockery
I swung myself as high as I could go
and I would try to see beyond
the Luton bungalow.

When my father lived in southern France
he would sit behind an easel,
teasing out the essence of a scene.
But something must have happened in between,
because it didn't tend to seem like he was talented,

his dedicated brushwork didn't show,
except for running round the skirting board
or touching up the pelmet
in the Luton bungalow.
But one spring I watched him kneeling
with a beanpole snapped in two,
it was a stick of old bamboo,
he was leant above the wet cement,
zig-zagging a line
engraving crazy paving,
engrossed in the design.
It was a work he failed to sign.
Imagined slab by zigzag slab
beneath the curving window out the front,
we should have hung out bunting,
let the beach-ball colours show
for all unsung potential
in each Luton Bungalow.
For all unused abilities.
For undiscovered skills.
For confetti which has not been cut,
no horseshoe shapes or frills.
For my mum's soft singing voice
it was her choice to hardly show.
For the wave she gave my dad each day
he went to sell his labour,
and especially for the moments she kept waving
though he'd passed around the corner.
For the waving which my father didn't know.
For the love inside
the Luton bungalow.

SHIFTING IT

In all the homes we lived in,
in all the times we lived in,
dancing – I didn't ever see my mum do none.
Sorry, let me say that better:
I never saw her non-dancing days undone.
But she used to put two rows of kisses gaily
on the cards I got each birthday,
like positions at the outset of a ceilidh.

On the autumn day of my birth itself,
when she pushed me out into the North London light,
I was heavy – nine-pounds-four of me.
I can't say what that is in metric,
for like my mother I am kilogrammatically incorrect.

Two further years in Islington smoke,
then further north to Luton
where space would be afforded
for the sister who would complement my brother
        and myself,
although we'd never get to compliment my sister.
It was a big shift – city to unknown town.
We relocated twice within its boundaries
before dad retired.

And then again, our suckling mum showed sense
    of adventure,
upping sticks to the sticks of Pucklechurch village
    near Bristol.
When housing needs contracted with my college
    days in Bradford,
when my sister took her family to Yate,
those sticks were upped a final time,
a mobile home for her and dad,
their first home without rent or mortgage.
A great decision, and their delight.
You could say she wasn't much of a dancer
but to that I'd have to answer
that my mother was a mover, alright.

SMALL SISTER

Small sister,
for the record
I was hiss.
I was mean and undermining.
I was the cloud that needed lining
and I stopped sun from shining.
Small sister,
I was the blister on your bliss.
In your kiss,
I was the Glasgow.

STICK MAN

Before you set to
with that thin bamboo,
you always asked us if we knew
why you were caning us.
One boy was told to go to you for treatment,
because his own teacher couldn't hit him
        hard enough.
He got your usual question,
'You know why I'm doing this?'
Absentmindedly the boy answered, 'Yes, Miss.'

Whenever you overshot your informed target
the stick would make a flappy sound
against your trouser leg
although such errors did not count
towards the canee's allotted amount.
You always gave us the full whack.

But then, you touched us in a softer way,
day after day, a clutch of your favourite poems,
always the same ones, in the same order.
And I thank you for banging in
that bing bang bongo lingo,
I'm grateful to you for hammering home

those gems in the wordpile,
that jawed magic.
And I'll remember you, if I can,
without your stick.
You were a man
with severe teaching difficulties.

THAILAND 2001

We gently rock
on the train out of Bangkok.
The Buddhist monk beside me is calm
    and approachable.
He has an orange cloth lying on his lap.
I presume it is related to the chap's belief,
playing some part in his praying
and devotion.
I feel that to enquire is not out of place.
I indicate the cloth,
gesturing, 'This thing – what is it for?'
He motions, that it is for wiping his sweaty face.

THE CLIMB

Some years back now, I was performing on the boards, amidst the swarming of the Edinburgh Festival, when a note was left for me at the theatre box-office: 'Don't do your show on Thursday. Meet me up Arthur's Seat.' It was signed, A. Potato.

There is something about this festival which generates over and above the usual level of communication between strangers. Everyone is very intent on their own thing, but the whole thing is very much everybody's, the communication channels are open.

I showed the potato instruction to a friend who had recently joined me in the flat which I had rented for the festival's duration. He said that if I did decide to find A. Potato on Thursday, I shouldn't go alone. I studied the writing once more. A sudden inspiration! I would lead the audience up the crag of Arthur's Seat for the promised meeting with this fleeting vegetable personage.

Thursday comes, I explain to my crowd that they have the option of the usual show, or the Potato adventure. Everyone opts for the unknown. There are eleven of them. Numbers have been gradually building – twelve with my friend. It's the last festival firework Thursday. Outside the venue, the sky is peppered with sparkling. Like these fire-works, we are going upwards. As our group hurries darkly across The Meadows, I have a happy and immense sense of illuminating possibility.

During the march, I retain the leader entertainer role, scattering festival anecdotes as we go, but as the climb gets harder, my words become fewer. Light is provided by some cheap garden torches which I had the forethought to purchase. We press on, passing shadowy firework spectators on well-appointed vantages. Finally, we approach the pinnacle.

At the top, a figure sits alone. With the group in tow, I approach.

'Excuse me, you're not A. Potato, are you?' I ask.

The figure turns into my torchlight. Immediately, I am struck by the distinctive jacket.

TONY AND THE FISH

The tale I want to tell
started in this seaside town's Montpelier Road
in 1978.
My mate Tony and myself went out
to walk beside the seaside,
the moon a newly minted coin.
And something on a concrete groyne was shining.
Tony said to me, 'It's a fish!'
Further inspection proved that no correction
    was required.
It was a fish.
And we guessed the lashing killed it
when the splashing tide had spilled it,
this, our bloody, blinding finding
without fishing or a fee.
We got the benefit in Brighton
from the lightening of the ocean's load
and we took that midnight mackerel back
to make tomorrow's tea.

TRAMPING

In New Zealand, rather than hiking, rambling, or fell-walking, one goes Tramping. For me, this conjures a deeper, more committed relationship with what's beneath your feet. A greater determination to connect.

Tramping, I'm going tramping
I feel like I've been going in reverse.
I'm going tramping
I need revamping
I've had my eyes upon my purse
not the horizon.
Tramping, I'm going tramping
I am champing at the bit
to hit the back-pack track
to let my footfall,
not so fretful,
to spread my tread
beyond the car-wheel clamping.
I'm going to put my foot down,
I'm going stamping ground
looking up into the come-what-daylight,
night-sky-lamping,
I'm going tramping.
Moorland, mountain, gorges, gorses,

marching with the world's charmed forces.
Over the moon,
under the moonshine,
under the sunshine,
over many an unmanicured mile,
tramping,
I'm going tramping,
for too long I've been cramping
my own smile.

23.1.00: 11.40 A.M.

Watching a video of yesternight's edition of 'Match of the Day', with my daughter.

She is looking out for me on the screen. She wants to know where I am. I explain that I was at another match. She says she wants me to go to the one where I can be on the telly. I say that it is hard to pick out people, in the crowd on the telly, I point to the herds of faces in their places in the stand.

'Why can't you go on the grass bit?' she demands. I shake my head. She does not give up.

'Pleeeeease?!'

'I can't,' I explain, 'I'm forty-six!'

She asks if I can do it when I'm forty-seven.

2B 2½

In the brasserie for breakfast
the artist puts his pencil
in her small and restless hand.
Pulling over a serviette
he says to get drawing.
The child gets drawing,
but over and beyond the designated area.
The table is now marked with lead.
No, not on the table, says the artist,
only draw on the paper.
And the bread.

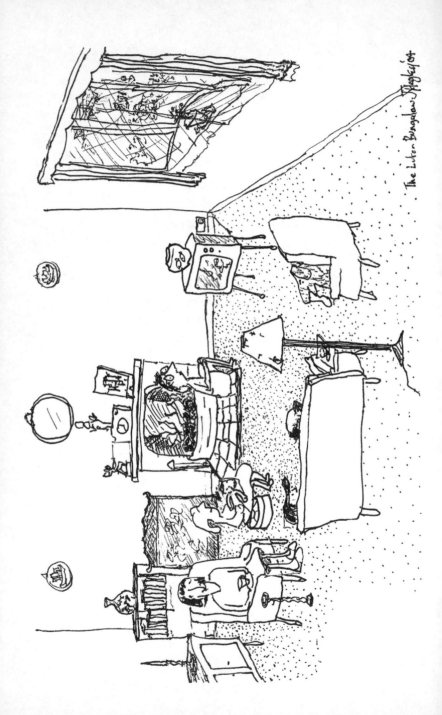

The Liter Bungalow. Hagley '04

WAY OUT

It's around 1965 or six
there's what they call pebble-dash over the bricks.
There's mum, dad and Angela, Marcel and me,
we're watching the telly
we've rented and like to surround of a night
with silence and slippers, with tea and delight.
My sister is grateful, she's staying up late
and so is her dolly,
I'm sat by the grate.
My brother and father together recline.
The few books we have stand up proudly in line.
Hunter, the doggie, is chewing a sock,
my brother's new trophy is stood by the clock,
it's a Wednesday, I think,
and outside it is wet,
but more worthy of mention,
behind the TV set
a tunnel's appeared in the wall.
It seems only me and mother can see it
and we shall investigate rather than flee it.

First she will put down her tea,
then it's into the tunnel
with mummy and me.

And once we've got used to the darkness
the eyes of my mother will fall
on some chewing gum stuck to the wall.
It makes her disgruntled,
I tell her to calm,
it's unsightly perhaps, but it does us no harm.
At the end of the tunnel
we look out to sea.
An enormous fig roll
is out strolling the tide.
My mother decides it is daft,
it should have a boat or a raft.
Looking around,
she says don't use the deckchairs,
they charge you a pound each.
There's a monk chewing gum,
there's my mum in her slippers,
there's me in my newly darned socks.
She goes to a telescope,
puts in a penny,
and shows me some steps
reaching right to the top of the rocks.
They remind me of stairs up which once we would go
long before life in the bungalow,
where I went up to bed in my mother's embrace.
We had a cat in that house, which was wild,
which I wanted to keep for the rest of my childhood,
which my dad caught
and brought to the van as we left
but it clawed its way out of the hessian sack,
then it ran back and it made me bereft.

That cat and the closeness I had with my mother
are two things I didn't retain.
With the cat, that is that,
but I say to my Mum,
'Come and squeeze me
please hold me, the way that you did when you
carried me up,'
and she does and she does and she does and she does
and she does
and she doesn't refrain.

73

WILD BUNCH

As a child
my dad called me various names.
A Bunch of M'galoop was my favourite.
Not a Bunch of M'galoops,
no, just the one …
you can't have a bunch of one,
can you?
Unless you're just having fun.
And we were.
It sounded like a feast
for an unusual African beast.
An animal whose life was free.
An astonishing creature,
whose eyes were pools
in which fools could see
the infinite
without it being scary.

ZANZIBAR

Knowing of my association
with spectacles
through song
and oration,
Help the Aged, the charity,
asked if I might have a pair
to spare
to provide clarity
for someone, in what I referred to
as the blurred world.

The next batch
for dispatch
would include the millionth donation
and it might help in the publicity line
if that millionth pair was mine.

And so I'd take the spectacles afar:
to Zanzibar.

*

We are met at the airport by Mr Abdul and Dr Issa. Before
we drive off, I realise I am without my mandolin. There

has been a mandolincident. I think it's at the airport in Nairobi, but maybe it is on the plane? I am assured it will be found and returned. Mr Abdul says it is an omen of adventure.

We are to visit, immediately, the eye hospital where Dr Issa holds his practice. Mr Abdul is our chaperone, and a representative of Help Age International, which oversees distribution of overseas spectacles collected by Help the Aged. His work is with the over-fifties.

*

> So fifty is the rift
> between young and old,
> a line soon to be crossed by this poet.
> I may cross it,
> I hope not to toe it.

*

The eye hospital is an eye opener: I'm shocked at the ancient nature of the equipment; the operating theatre roof is not weatherproof.

In the hospital workshop I see again my donated spectacles: the spectacles I attempted to escape from in Covent Garden Piazza in 1982, through which I saw my first Edinburgh Festival audience the following year, through which I saw in the new year of 1984 and through which I saw my father's native land of France for the first time. The spectacles through which I read the letter from the other residents of the shared house in East London demanding I leave, because I was terminally anti-social. These are the spectacles through which I am hoping someone on a continent of leopards will clearly see the spots of their own experience.

*

I am so impressed
to see them brought back to their best.
The frames
are all wobbly
and playing their own games.
But I'm told this can be mended
and I see the wobble ended.
Screws are turned and rivets tightened.
I look on and am enlightened.

*

Browsing in the lively night-time market on the esplanade, I told one eager salesman that I did not want the cloth he was wielding, I wanted a drum. This, I thought, might add some local colour to my verses. A drum was found from the stall of a colleague and the vendor and I locked horns in price fixing. A process which I later labelled Zanzibartering – getting 'to barter' and 'to haggle' confused.

*

I have a poem called *My Doggie Don't Wear Glasses*. During the process of poem translation it has been explained that my doggie not wearing spectacles is not best suited to the religion of the local audience, who would not place such an animal in the household. It has been suggested I might say instead that it is my *ox* which does not wear spectacles. I decide to omit the poem – doubting that the people of Zanzibar have a convention of people looking like their oxen.

*

Our itinerary includes a presentation of spectacles at a large local gathering. Music will be provided by myself and other local players under a mango tree. We will encounter a villager of whom I am told, 'She is the recipient of the glasses you sent'. I'm glad that my glasses have come into the ball park – the eye ball park.

*

I buy a traditional hat
that has no brim
a bit like a fez, but shorter
and a t-shirt
with the basics of Swahili
for my daughter.

*

We leave the hotel sharp at seven a.m. to meet with the musicians at eight. Sustenance is provided for the journey in the form of fruit platters and sandwiches. Dr Issa, who takes the wheel of our small vehicle, drives us apace, slaloming the road's many pot holes.

> A long way from Islington and Hackney
> in the passenger seat
> motoring forth
> to the island's north.
> In the cranking heat
> through the morning mist,
> in the leaf-locked shade
> the bicycles evade
> the tarmac acne.

On arrival at the Eye Ball we are glad to hear the drums already resonating around the designated mango tree. I set about my own drum to strike up acquaintance in the common language of rhythm.

*

> Here we are alfresco
> underneath the mango
> nearer to the Congo
> than we are to Tesco,
> playing with the combo
> I am on my bongo
> but I am no Ringo
> Starr.

Playing with the combo
of another lingo,
more than a momento
this is the tabasco
on my trip
to Zanzibar.

*

Tuta fanya nini na miwani ya Babu?
What we gonna to do about granddad's glasses?
The simple answer is we'll hand them on
now that granddad's dancing days are done,
and so the baton passes
from one to another
to a brother
or a sister in arms,
(these alms).

*

We are
gathered round in Zanzibar
to bear witness to the glasses,
to make what passes
to the brain not be all blurry.
I go running round the circle
of the people of the village
who will see the glasses given
and with singing and with drumming
we all celebrate the coming

of the clearness of the seeing
in the sun.
And I swing around the spectacles.
I'm doting on the potency
of what will soon be given
to the swelling of Swahili,
for the elder who may really
wish I'd stop mucking about
and get it done.

*

There's some debate over the origin of the word Zanzibar,
whether it comes from the words Zinj el Barr – land of
black people – or Zayn za'l barr – fair is this land. In this
matter the flattery of the latter is not unreasonable.

*

I've sensed the sacred
I've felt the sea
I've helped the aged
and they've helped me.
I've rhymed some poems
I've written some prose
and I've been bitten
by a lot of mosquitoes,
and I've heard
enough to see
that the people of Zanzibar
have the sharpest sense of what they are

and what they ought,
the world I referred to once as blurred
is not the way I thought.

*

In Zanzibar,
the place
where Stanley presumed
he had discovered Livingstone,
I assumed
an impoverished populace.
Experience has adjusted my view.
Alongside humble homes and rudimentary roads
I met with giving, respect and grace,
came face to face
with dignity and control:
corrected vision does not come solely
from a glasses' case.

*

In search of sweets and biscuits, we walk through the hubbubbing streets, in the old town's hub of street market. I intimate that I am in need of some lighter footwear, as the heavy shoes and fisherman style socks I have brought with me are becoming increasingly irksome.

After the purchasing of sandals, I am aware of the fungal growth which has been troubling my outer left foot.

I come across an ancient stall displaying various species

of tree bark. Mr Marco Pello informs me that this is a traditional medicine stall. I remove my new sandals and show the patron my old ailment. He recommends I go to a chemist.

ZEN DAD

When I asked my father why he'd stopped painting
he told me, 'You children are my paintings now.'
The brushes down, he became a gardening man.
Moving homes, there were the various wildernesses
        for him to tame.
Thick, brick-a-bramble challenges,
which he brought into line.
Brushing with nature,
brushing the paths,
blushing with effort.
Pinks and nasturtiums,
string and bamboo,
border plants and beans,
the fork and the trowel,
trod and turned
long beyond daylight.
'I don't know what he does out there,'
said mum.
If you'd really pressed her
she'd have guessed, I think:
time alone,
the creation of order,
communion with God.
On the last occasion

he came indoors, complaining of pains in the chest.
Mum suggested he'd best lie down.
'I'll just go and put my tools away,' he answered,
which he did.
Back in again,
lying on the sofa
he slipped away from the world and the woman
he loved as one.
The job
well and truly,
and very tidily,
done.